Oxford
Reading
Tree

Myself

FACT
FINDERS

All kinds of toys

Roderick Hunt

Oxford University Press

The children have lots of toys.

Some are old, and some are new.

What kinds of toys are there?

Contents

Model toys

Many toys are models.

These are old model cars.

The real cars looked like these.

Models look like the real thing.

This is a model farm.

It looks like a real farm.

Clockwork toys

Clockwork
motor

These toys are old.

They all have clockwork motors.

Clockwork motors have a key.

The key winds the motor up.

This makes the motor go.

These new toys have clockwork motors.

Battery toys

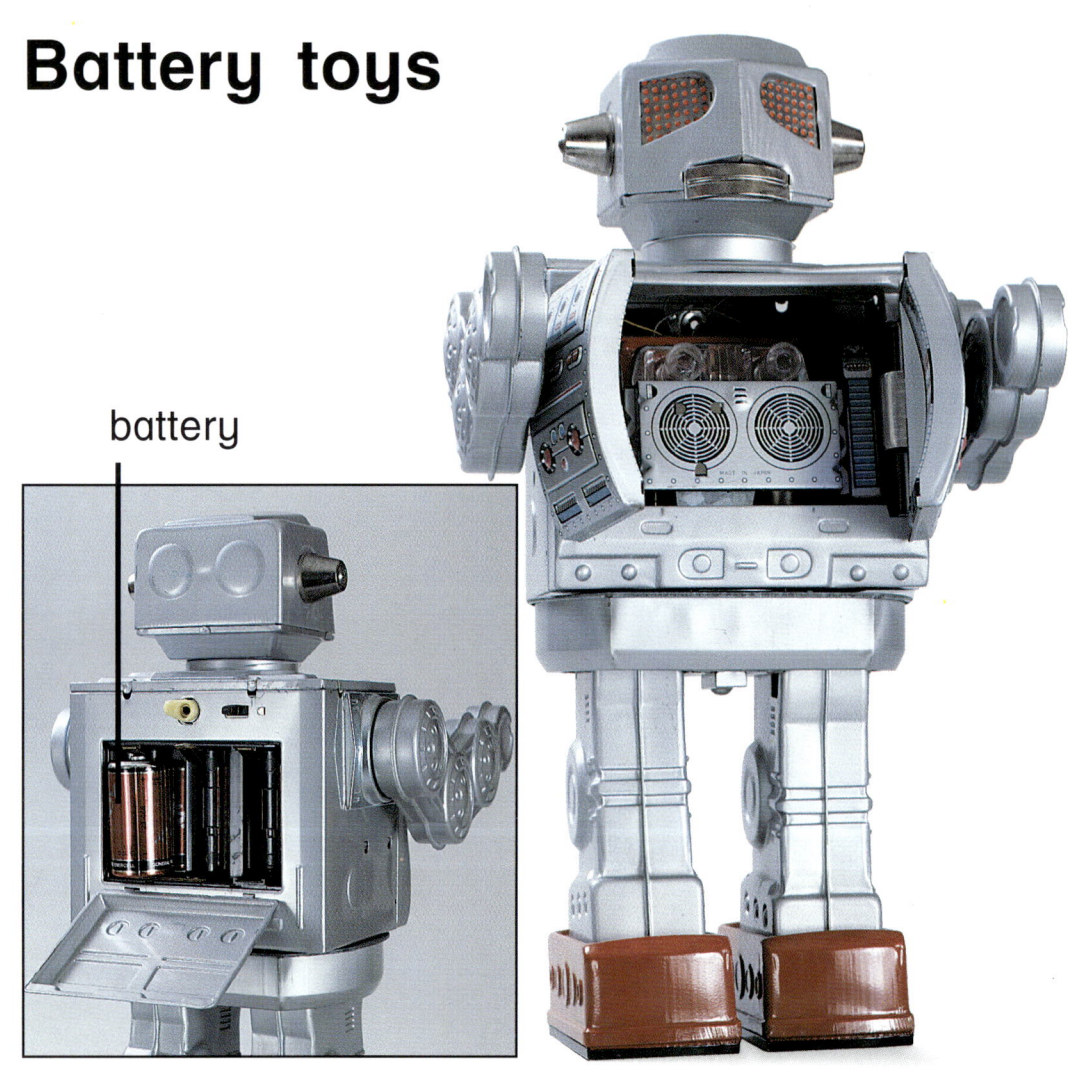

battery

These old toys have motors.

The motors need batteries.

The batteries make them work.

This new toy guitar has batteries, too.
The guitar plays a tune when
you press the buttons.

Dolls

These old dolls have china heads.

The heads break easily.

The dolls have soft bodies.

This new doll is made of plastic.

It moves when you press a button.

It has a battery motor inside.

Construction toys

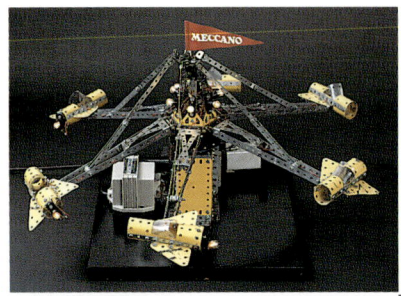

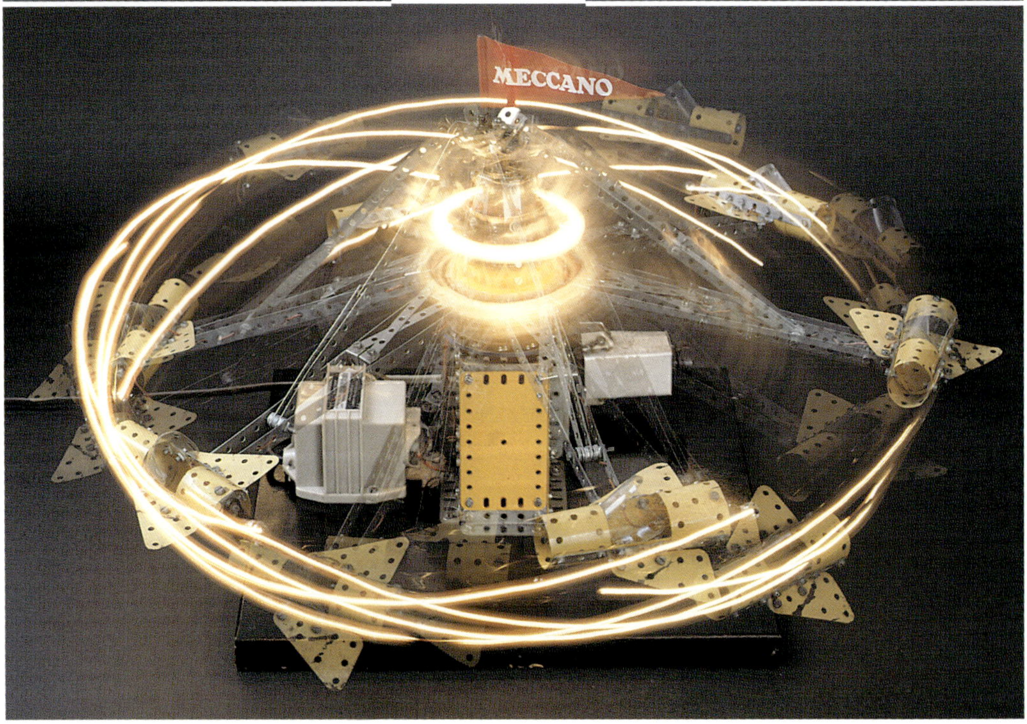

You can build things with
construction toys.
This old toy is made from Meccano.

This new toy is made from Lego.
Construction toys have not
changed much.

Games

These are board games.

Children played them long ago.

They still play them today.

Computer games are new.

Children didn't have them long ago.

Index

battery toy   8–9, 11

clockwork toy   6–7

construction toy   12–13

doll   10–11

game   14–15

model   4–5

Oxford University Press, Great Clarendon Street,
Oxford OX2 6DP
© Oxford University Press
All rights reserved

First published by Oxford University Press 1994
Reprinted 1995, 1997, 1998 (twice), 2001 (twice)
ISBN 0 19 916633 1

Available in packs
Myself pack (one of each title)
ISBN 0 19 916634 X
Myself class pack (six of each title)
ISBN 0 19 916635 8

Teacher's Guide 1   ISBN 0 19 916670 6

Acknowledgements

The publisher would like to thank the following for the help
in supplying items for photography: The Early Learning
Centre (cover, 5, 7 [top left], 13, 14 [bottom]); LEGO
(cover, 13); The London Toy and Model Museum, 21/23
Craven Hill, London W2 3EN (cover, 4, 6, 8, 10, 12)
Photographs by: Martin Sookias
Illustrated by: Alex Brychta (p2)

Printed in China